HORSES

2023 DIARY

THIS DIARY BELONGS TO...

Name:
....

Address:
....

....

....

Postcode:
....

Telephone:
....

Work:
....

Mobile:
....

Fax:
....

E-mail:
....

IN AN EMERGENCY...

Name:
....

Address:
....

....

....

Postcode:
....

Telephone:
....

Work:
....

Mobile:
....

CONTACT NUMBERS

Name:

Tel:

Name:

Tel:

Name:

Tel:

Name:

Tel:

Name:

Tel:

Name:

Tel:

Name:

Tel:

Name:

Tel:

Name:

Tel:

Name:

Tel:

Name:

Tel:

CONTACT NUMBERS

Name:

Tel:

Name:

Tel:

Name:

Tel:

Name:

Tel:

Name:

Tel:

Name:

Tel:

Name:

Tel:

Name:

Tel:

Name:

Tel:

Name:

Tel:

Name:

Tel:

CONTACT NUMBERS

Name:

Tel:

Name:

Tel:

Name:

Tel:

Name:

Tel:

Name:

Tel:

Name:

Tel:

Name:

Tel:

Name:

Tel:

Name:

Tel:

Name:

Tel:

Name:

Tel:

CONVERSIONS

1 in = 2.54 cm	$1\ in^2 = 6.4516\ cm^2$
1 cm = 0.3937 in	$1\ cm^2 = 0.155\ in^2$
1 ft = 0.3048 m	$1\ ft^2 = 0.0929\ m^2$
1 m = 3.2808 ft	$1\ m^2 = 10.7639\ ft^2$
1 yd = 0.9144 m	$1\ mile^2 = 2.59\ km^2$
1 m = 1.0936 yd	$1\ km^2 = 0.3861\ miles^2$
1 mile = 1.6093 km	1 acre = 0.4047 ha
1 km = 0.6214 miles	1 ha = 2.471 acres

$1\ in^3 = 16.387\ cm^3$	1 UK gal = 4.546 l
$1\ cm^3 = 0.06102\ in^3$	1 l = 0.22 UK gal
$1\ ft^3 = 0.02832\ m^3$	1 oz = 28.3495 g
$1\ m^3 = 35.3147\ ft^3$	1 g = 0.03527 oz
$1\ yd^3 = 0.76456\ m^3$	1 lb = 453.59 g
$1\ m^3 = 1.30795\ yd^3$	1 g = 0.002205 lb
1 US gal = 3.7854 l	1 kg = 2.2046 lb
1 l = 0.2642 US gal	1 t (long) = 1016.0469 kg
1 US gal = 0.8327 UK gal	1 kg = 0.00098 t (long)

USEFUL WEBSITES

AA	www.theaa.com
RAC	www.rac.co.uk
Green Flag	www.greenflag.com
Eurotunnel	www.eurotunnel.com
Eurostar	www.eurostar.com
London Travel Info	www.tfl.gov.uk
National Rail	www.nationalrail.co.uk
National Express Coaches	www.nationalexpress.com
British Airways	www.britishairways.com
Virgin	www.virginatlantic.com
EasyJet	www.easyjet.com
Ryanair	www.ryanair.com
Avis	www.avis.co.uk
Europcar	www.europcar.co.uk
Hertz	www.hertz.co.uk
UK Traffic Info	www.gov.uk/traffic-information
Road Maps (Worldwide)	www.google.com/maps
Road Maps (UK)	www.streetmap.co.uk
World Time Zones	www.worldtimezone.com

USEFUL CONTACTS

Tourist Information:
www.visitbritain.com
Telephone: 020 7578 1000

Healthcare:
www.nhs.uk
Telephone: 111 (non-emergency calls)
Telephone: 999 (emergency calls)

Police:
www.police.uk
Telephone: 101 (non-emergency calls)
Telephone: 999 (emergency calls)

Government Services:
www.gov.uk

Doctor:

Dentist:

Hospital:

Local Police Station:

Local Council:

Medical Information:

Car Insurance:

Car Breakdown:

NOTABLE DATES

January

1	Sun	New Year's Day
2	Mon	Holiday (UK, R. of Ireland, USA, CAN, AUS, NZL)
3	Tue	Holiday (SCT, NZL)
16	Mon	Martin Luther King, Jr. Day (Holiday USA)
22	Sun	Chinese New Year - Year of the Rabbit
25	Wed	Burns Night (SCT)
26	Thu	Australia Day (Holiday AUS)

February

6	Mon	Waitangi Day (Holiday NZL)
14	Tue	St Valentine's Day
20	Mon	Presidents' Day (Holiday USA)
21	Tue	Shrove Tuesday
22	Wed	Ash Wednesday

March

1	Wed	St David's Day
17	Fri	St Patrick's Day (Holiday N. Ireland, R. of Ireland)
19	Sun	Mothering Sunday (UK, R. of Ireland)
22	Wed	Ramadan Begins at Sundown
26	Sun	British Summer Time begins

April

5	Wed	Passover Begins at Sundown
7	Fri	Good Friday (Holiday UK, CAN, AUS, NZL)
9	Sun	Easter Sunday
10	Mon	Easter Monday (Holiday UK except SCT, R. of Ireland, CAN, AUS, NZL)
13	Thu	Passover Ends at Sundown
21	Fri	Eid al-Fitr Begins at Sundown
23	Sun	St George's Day
25	Tue	Anzac Day (Holiday AUS, NZL)

May

1	Mon	Holiday (UK, R. of Ireland)
14	Sun	Mother's Day (USA, CAN, AUS, NZL)
22	Mon	Victoria Day (Holiday CAN)
29	Mon	Holiday (UK) Memorial Day (Holiday USA)

June

5	Mon	Holiday (R. of Ireland) Queen's Birthday (Holiday NZL)
18	Sun	Father's Day (UK, R. of Ireland, USA, CAN)
19	Mon	Juneteenth (Holiday USA)

NOTABLE DATES

July
1	Sat	Canada Day (Holiday CAN)
4	Tue	Independence Day (Holiday USA)
12	Wed	Battle of the Boyne (Holiday N. Ireland)

August
7	Mon	Holiday (SCT, R. of Ireland)
28	Mon	Holiday (UK except SCT)

September
3	Sun	Father's Day (AUS, NZL)
4	Mon	Labor Day (Holiday USA)
		Labour Day (Holiday CAN)

October
9	Mon	Columbus Day (Holiday USA)
		Thanksgiving Day (Holiday CAN)
23	Mon	Labour Day (Holiday NZL)
29	Sun	British Summer Time ends
30	Mon	Holiday (R. of Ireland)
31	Tue	Hallowe'en

November
5	Sun	Bonfire Night
10	Fri	Holiday (USA)
11	Sat	Veterans Day (USA)
		Remembrance Day (Holiday CAN)
12	Sun	Remembrance Sunday (UK)
		Diwali
23	Thu	Thanksgiving Day (Holiday USA)
30	Thu	St Andrew's Day (Holiday SCT)

December
24	Sun	Christmas Eve
25	Mon	Christmas Day (Holiday UK, R. of Ireland, USA, CAN, AUS, NZL)
26	Tue	Boxing Day, St Stephen's Day (Holiday UK, R. of Ireland, CAN, AUS, NZL)
31	Sun	New Year's Eve

2022 CALENDAR

	JANUARY	FEBRUARY	MARCH	APRIL
Monday	31 3 10 17 24	7 14 21 28	7 14 21 28	4 11 18 25
Tuesday	4 11 18 25	1 8 15 22	1 8 15 22 29	5 12 19 26
Wednesday	5 12 19 26	2 9 16 23	2 9 16 23 30	6 13 20 27
Thursday	6 13 20 27	3 10 17 24	3 10 17 24 31	7 14 21 28
Friday	7 14 21 28	4 11 18 25	4 11 18 25	1 8 15 22 29
Saturday	1 8 15 22 29	5 12 19 26	5 12 19 26	2 9 16 23 30
Sunday	2 9 16 23 30	6 13 20 27	6 13 20 27	3 10 17 24

	MAY	JUNE	JULY	AUGUST
Monday	30 2 9 16 23	6 13 20 27	4 11 18 25	1 8 15 22 29
Tuesday	31 3 10 17 24	7 14 21 28	5 12 19 26	2 9 16 23 30
Wednesday	4 11 18 25	1 8 15 22 29	6 13 20 27	3 10 17 24 31
Thursday	5 12 19 26	2 9 16 23 30	7 14 21 28	4 11 18 25
Friday	6 13 20 27	3 10 17 24	1 8 15 22 29	5 12 19 26
Saturday	7 14 21 28	4 11 18 25	2 9 16 23 30	6 13 20 27
Sunday	1 8 15 22 29	5 12 19 26	3 10 17 24 31	7 14 21 28

	SEPTEMBER	OCTOBER	NOVEMBER	DECEMBER
Monday	5 12 19 26	31 3 10 17 24	7 14 21 28	5 12 19 26
Tuesday	6 13 20 27	4 11 18 25	1 8 15 22 29	6 13 20 27
Wednesday	7 14 21 28	5 12 19 26	2 9 16 23 30	7 14 21 28
Thursday	1 8 15 22 29	6 13 20 27	3 10 17 24	1 8 15 22 29
Friday	2 9 16 23 30	7 14 21 28	4 11 18 25	2 9 16 23 30
Saturday	3 10 17 24	1 8 15 22 29	5 12 19 26	3 10 17 24 31
Sunday	4 11 18 25	2 9 16 23 30	6 13 20 27	4 11 18 25

2024 CALENDAR

	JANUARY	FEBRUARY	MARCH	APRIL
Monday	1 8 15 22 29	5 12 19 26	4 11 18 25	1 8 15 22 29
Tuesday	2 9 16 23 30	6 13 20 27	5 12 19 26	2 9 16 23 30
Wednesday	3 10 17 24 31	7 14 21 28	6 13 20 27	3 10 17 24
Thursday	4 11 18 25	1 8 15 22 29	7 14 21 28	4 11 18 25
Friday	5 12 19 26	2 9 16 23	1 8 15 22 29	5 12 19 26
Saturday	6 13 20 27	3 10 17 24	2 9 16 23 30	6 13 20 27
Sunday	7 14 21 28	4 11 18 25	3 10 17 24 31	7 14 21 28

	MAY	JUNE	JULY	AUGUST
Monday	6 13 20 27	3 10 17 24	1 8 15 22 29	5 12 19 26
Tuesday	7 14 21 28	4 11 18 25	2 9 16 23 30	6 13 20 27
Wednesday	1 8 15 22 29	5 12 19 26	3 10 17 24 31	7 14 21 28
Thursday	2 9 16 23 30	6 13 20 27	4 11 18 25	1 8 15 22 29
Friday	3 10 17 24 31	7 14 21 28	5 12 19 26	2 9 16 23 30
Saturday	4 11 18 25	1 8 15 22 29	6 13 20 27	3 10 17 24 31
Sunday	5 12 19 26	2 9 16 23 30	7 14 21 28	4 11 18 25

	SEPTEMBER	OCTOBER	NOVEMBER	DECEMBER
Monday	30 2 9 16 23	7 14 21 28	4 11 18 25	30 2 9 16 23
Tuesday	3 10 17 24	1 8 15 22 29	5 12 19 26	31 3 10 17 24
Wednesday	4 11 18 25	2 9 16 23 30	6 13 20 27	4 11 18 25
Thursday	5 12 19 26	3 10 17 24 31	7 14 21 28	5 12 19 26
Friday	6 13 20 27	4 11 18 25	1 8 15 22 29	6 13 20 27
Saturday	7 14 21 28	5 12 19 26	2 9 16 23 30	7 14 21 28
Sunday	1 8 15 22 29	6 13 20 27	3 10 17 24	1 8 15 22 29

2023 CALENDAR

JANUARY

Monday	30	2	9	16	23
Tuesday	31	3	10	17	24
Wednesday		4	11	18	25
Thursday		5	12	19	26
Friday		6	13	20	27
Saturday		7	14	21	28
Sunday	1	8	15	22	29

FEBRUARY

Monday		6	13	20	27
Tuesday		7	14	21	28
Wednesday	1	8	15	22	
Thursday	2	9	16	23	
Friday	3	10	17	24	
Saturday	4	11	18	25	
Sunday	5	12	19	26	

MARCH

Monday		6	13	20	27
Tuesday		7	14	21	28
Wednesday	1	8	15	22	29
Thursday	2	9	16	23	30
Friday	3	10	17	24	31
Saturday	4	11	18	25	
Sunday	5	12	19	26	

APRIL

Monday		3	10	17	24
Tuesday		4	11	18	25
Wednesday		5	12	19	26
Thursday		6	13	20	27
Friday		7	14	21	28
Saturday	1	8	15	22	29
Sunday	2	9	16	23	30

MAY

Monday	1	8	15	22	29
Tuesday	2	9	16	23	30
Wednesday	3	10	17	24	31
Thursday	4	11	18	25	
Friday	5	12	19	26	
Saturday	6	13	20	27	
Sunday	7	14	21	28	

JUNE

Monday		5	12	19	26
Tuesday		6	13	20	27
Wednesday		7	14	21	28
Thursday	1	8	15	22	29
Friday	2	9	16	23	30
Saturday	3	10	17	24	
Sunday	4	11	18	25	

JULY

Monday	31	3	10	17	24
Tuesday		4	11	18	25
Wednesday		5	12	19	26
Thursday		6	13	20	27
Friday		7	14	21	28
Saturday	1	8	15	22	29
Sunday	2	9	16	23	30

AUGUST

Monday		7	14	21	28
Tuesday	1	8	15	22	29
Wednesday	2	9	16	23	30
Thursday	3	10	17	24	31
Friday	4	11	18	25	
Saturday	5	12	19	26	
Sunday	6	13	20	27	

SEPTEMBER

Monday		4	11	18	25
Tuesday		5	12	19	26
Wednesday		6	13	20	27
Thursday		7	14	21	28
Friday	1	8	15	22	29
Saturday	2	9	16	23	30
Sunday	3	10	17	24	

OCTOBER

Monday	30	2	9	16	23
Tuesday	31	3	10	17	24
Wednesday		4	11	18	25
Thursday		5	12	19	26
Friday		6	13	20	27
Saturday		7	14	21	28
Sunday	1	8	15	22	29

NOVEMBER

Monday		6	13	20	27
Tuesday		7	14	21	28
Wednesday	1	8	15	22	29
Thursday	2	9	16	23	30
Friday	3	10	17	24	
Saturday	4	11	18	25	
Sunday	5	12	19	26	

DECEMBER

Monday		4	11	18	25
Tuesday		5	12	19	26
Wednesday		6	13	20	27
Thursday		7	14	21	28
Friday	1	8	15	22	29
Saturday	2	9	16	23	30
Sunday	3	10	17	24	31

SD1-13-23

DEC 2022 – JAN 2023

MONDAY
26

Boxing Day, St Stephen's Day (Holiday UK, R. of Ireland, CAN, AUS, NZL)
Holiday (USA)

TUESDAY
27

Holiday (UK, R. of Ireland, CAN, AUS, NZL)

WEDNESDAY
28

THURSDAY
29

FRIDAY
30

◑

SATURDAY
31

New Year's Eve

SUNDAY
1

New Year's Day

JANUARY

MONDAY
2

Holiday (UK, R. of Ireland, USA, CAN, AUS, NZL)

TUESDAY
3

Holiday (SCT, NZL)

WEDNESDAY
4

THURSDAY
5

FRIDAY ○
6

SATURDAY
7

SUNDAY
8

JANUARY

MONDAY
9

TUESDAY
10

WEDNESDAY
11

THURSDAY
12

FRIDAY
13

SATURDAY
14

◑ SUNDAY
15

JANUARY

MONDAY
16

Martin Luther King, Jr. Day (Holiday USA)

TUESDAY
17

WEDNESDAY
18

THURSDAY
19

FRIDAY
20

SATURDAY
21   ●

SUNDAY
22

Chinese New Year - Year of the Rabbit

JANUARY

MONDAY
23

TUESDAY
24

WEDNESDAY
25

Burns Night (SCT)

THURSDAY
26

Australia Day (Holiday AUS)

FRIDAY
27

◑

SATURDAY
28

SUNDAY
29

JANUARY - FEBRUARY

MONDAY
30

TUESDAY
31

WEDNESDAY
1

THURSDAY
2

FRIDAY
3

SATURDAY
4

SUNDAY
5

○

FEBRUARY

MONDAY
6

Waitangi Day (Holiday NZL)

TUESDAY
7

WEDNESDAY
8

THURSDAY
9

FRIDAY
10

SATURDAY
11

SUNDAY
12

FEBRUARY

SD1-23-23

MONDAY
13

TUESDAY
14

St Valentine's Day
WEDNESDAY
15

THURSDAY
16

FRIDAY
17

SATURDAY
18

SUNDAY
19

FEBRUARY

MONDAY
20

●

Presidents' Day (Holiday USA)
....

TUESDAY
21

Shrove Tuesday
....

WEDNESDAY
22

Ash Wednesday
....

THURSDAY
23

....

FRIDAY
24

....

SATURDAY
25

....

SUNDAY
26

FEBRUARY - MARCH

◐

MONDAY
27

TUESDAY
28

WEDNESDAY
1

St David's Day
THURSDAY
2

FRIDAY
3

SATURDAY
4

SUNDAY
5

MARCH

MONDAY
6

TUESDAY
7 ○

WEDNESDAY
8

THURSDAY
9

FRIDAY
10

SATURDAY
11

SUNDAY
12

MARCH

MONDAY
13

TUESDAY
14

WEDNESDAY ◑
15

THURSDAY
16

FRIDAY
17

St Patrick's Day (Holiday N. Ireland, R. of Ireland)

SATURDAY
18

SUNDAY
19

Mothering Sunday (UK, R. of Ireland)

MARCH

MONDAY
20

TUESDAY
21

WEDNESDAY
22

Ramadan Begins at Sundown
THURSDAY
23

FRIDAY
24

SATURDAY
25

SUNDAY
26

British Summer Time begins

SD1-29-23

MARCH - APRIL

MONDAY
27

TUESDAY
28

WEDNESDAY
29   ◑

THURSDAY
30

FRIDAY
31

SATURDAY
1

SUNDAY
2

APRIL

MONDAY
3

TUESDAY
4

WEDNESDAY
5

Passover Begins at Sundown

THURSDAY
6   ○

FRIDAY
7

Good Friday (Holiday UK, CAN, AUS, NZL)

SATURDAY
8

SUNDAY
9

Easter Sunday

SD1-32-23

APRIL

MONDAY
10

Easter Monday (Holiday UK except SCT, R. of Ireland, CAN, AUS, NZL)

TUESDAY
11

WEDNESDAY
12

◖ THURSDAY
13

Passover Ends at Sundown

FRIDAY
14

SATURDAY
15

SUNDAY
16

APRIL

MONDAY
17

TUESDAY
18

WEDNESDAY
19

THURSDAY
20

●

FRIDAY
21

Eid al-Fitr Begins at Sundown

SATURDAY
22

SUNDAY
23

St George's Day

MONDAY
24

TUESDAY
25

Anzac Day (Holiday AUS, NZL)
WEDNESDAY
26

◑
THURSDAY
27

FRIDAY
28

SATURDAY
29

SUNDAY
30

MAY

MONDAY
1

Holiday (UK, R. of Ireland)

TUESDAY
2

WEDNESDAY
3

THURSDAY
4

FRIDAY
5

○

SATURDAY
6

SUNDAY
7

MAY

MONDAY
8

TUESDAY
9

WEDNESDAY
10

THURSDAY
11

FRIDAY   ☽
12

SATURDAY
13

SUNDAY
14

Mother's Day (USA, CAN, AUS, NZL)

MAY

MONDAY
15

TUESDAY
16

WEDNESDAY
17

THURSDAY
18

●

FRIDAY
19

SATURDAY
20

SUNDAY
21

MAY

MONDAY
22

Victoria Day (Holiday CAN)

TUESDAY
23

WEDNESDAY
24

THURSDAY
25

FRIDAY
26

SATURDAY ◐
27

SUNDAY
28

MAY - JUNE

MONDAY
29

Holiday (UK)
Memorial Day (Holiday USA)

TUESDAY
30

WEDNESDAY
31

THURSDAY
1

FRIDAY
2

SATURDAY
3

○ SUNDAY
4

JUNE

MONDAY
5

Holiday (R. of Ireland)
Queen's Birthday (Holiday NZL)

TUESDAY
6

WEDNESDAY
7

THURSDAY
8

FRIDAY
9

SATURDAY
10

SUNDAY
11

JUNE

MONDAY
12

TUESDAY
13

WEDNESDAY
14

THURSDAY
15

FRIDAY
16

SATURDAY
17

SUNDAY
18

●

Father's Day (UK, R. of Ireland, USA, CAN)

SD1-44-23

JUNE

MONDAY
19

Juneteenth (Holiday USA)

TUESDAY
20

WEDNESDAY
21

THURSDAY
22

FRIDAY
23

SATURDAY
24

SUNDAY
25

JUNE – JULY

MONDAY
26

TUESDAY
27

WEDNESDAY
28

THURSDAY
29

FRIDAY
30

SATURDAY
1

Canada Day (Holiday CAN)

SUNDAY
2

JULY

MONDAY ○
3

TUESDAY
4

Independence Day (Holiday USA)

WEDNESDAY
5

THURSDAY
6

FRIDAY
7

SATURDAY
8

SUNDAY
9

JULY

◐
MONDAY
10

TUESDAY
11

WEDNESDAY
12

Battle of the Boyne (Holiday N. Ireland)
THURSDAY
13

FRIDAY
14

SATURDAY
15

SUNDAY
16

SD1-49-23

JULY

MONDAY
17   ●

TUESDAY
18

WEDNESDAY
19

THURSDAY
20

FRIDAY
21

SATURDAY
22

SUNDAY
23

MONDAY
24

TUESDAY
25

WEDNESDAY
26

THURSDAY
27

FRIDAY
28

SATURDAY
29

SUNDAY
30

JULY - AUGUST

MONDAY
31

TUESDAY
1   ○

WEDNESDAY
2

THURSDAY
3

FRIDAY
4

SATURDAY
5

SUNDAY
6

AUGUST

MONDAY
7

Holiday (SCT, R. of Ireland)

TUESDAY ◑
8

WEDNESDAY
9

THURSDAY
10

FRIDAY
11

SATURDAY
12

SUNDAY
13

AUGUST

MONDAY
14

TUESDAY
15

● WEDNESDAY
16

THURSDAY
17

FRIDAY
18

SATURDAY
19

SUNDAY
20

AUGUST

MONDAY
21

TUESDAY
22

WEDNESDAY
23

THURSDAY
24

FRIDAY
25

SATURDAY
26

SUNDAY
27

AUGUST - SEPTEMBER

MONDAY
28

Holiday (UK except SCT)

TUESDAY
29

WEDNESDAY
30

○ THURSDAY
31

FRIDAY
1

SATURDAY
2

SUNDAY
3

Father's Day (AUS, NZL)

SD1-57-23

SEPTEMBER

MONDAY
4

Labor Day (Holiday USA)
Labour Day (Holiday CAN)

TUESDAY
5

WEDNESDAY ◑
6

THURSDAY
7

FRIDAY
8

SATURDAY
9

SUNDAY
10

SEPTEMBER

MONDAY
11

TUESDAY
12

WEDNESDAY
13

THURSDAY
14

FRIDAY
15
●

SATURDAY
16

SUNDAY
17

SEPTEMBER

MONDAY
18

TUESDAY
19

WEDNESDAY
20

THURSDAY
21

◐ FRIDAY
22

SATURDAY
23

SUNDAY
24

SEPTEMBER - OCTOBER

MONDAY
25

TUESDAY
26

WEDNESDAY
27

THURSDAY
28

FRIDAY
29   ○

SATURDAY
30

SUNDAY
1

OCTOBER

MONDAY
2

TUESDAY
3

WEDNESDAY
4

THURSDAY
5

FRIDAY
6

SATURDAY
7

SUNDAY
8

OCTOBER

Columbus Day (Holiday USA)
Thanksgiving Day (Holiday CAN)

TUESDAY
10

WEDNESDAY
11

THURSDAY
12

FRIDAY
13

SATURDAY
14

SUNDAY
15

OCTOBER

MONDAY
16

TUESDAY
17

WEDNESDAY
18

THURSDAY
19

FRIDAY
20

SATURDAY
21

SUNDAY
22

◐

OCTOBER

MONDAY
23

TUESDAY
24

WEDNESDAY
25

THURSDAY
26

FRIDAY
27

○

SATURDAY
28

SUNDAY
29

British Summer Time ends

OCTOBER – NOVEMBER

MONDAY
30

Holiday (R. of Ireland)

TUESDAY
31

Hallowe'en

WEDNESDAY
1

THURSDAY
2

FRIDAY
3

SATURDAY
4

SUNDAY
5

◑

Bonfire Night

NOVEMBER

MONDAY
6

TUESDAY
7

WEDNESDAY
8

THURSDAY
9

FRIDAY
10

Holiday (USA)

SATURDAY
11

Veterans Day (USA)
Remembrance Day (Holiday CAN)

SUNDAY
12

Remembrance Sunday (UK)
Diwali

NOVEMBER

MONDAY
13

TUESDAY
14

WEDNESDAY
15

THURSDAY
16

FRIDAY
17

SATURDAY
18

SUNDAY
19

NOVEMBER

MONDAY
20

TUESDAY
21

WEDNESDAY
22

THURSDAY
23

Thanksgiving Day (Holiday USA)

FRIDAY
24

SATURDAY
25

SUNDAY
26

NOVEMBER - DECEMBER

○

MONDAY
27

TUESDAY
28

WEDNESDAY
29

THURSDAY
30

St Andrew's Day (Holiday SCT)

FRIDAY
1

SATURDAY
2

SUNDAY
3

DECEMBER

MONDAY
4

TUESDAY ◑
5

WEDNESDAY
6

THURSDAY
7

FRIDAY
8

SATURDAY
9

SUNDAY
10

DECEMBER

MONDAY
11

TUESDAY
12
●

WEDNESDAY
13

THURSDAY
14

FRIDAY
15

SATURDAY
16

SUNDAY
17

DECEMBER

MONDAY
18

TUESDAY
19

WEDNESDAY
20

THURSDAY
21

FRIDAY
22

SATURDAY
23

SUNDAY
24

Christmas Eve

DECEMBER

MONDAY
25

Christmas Day (Holiday UK, R. of Ireland, USA, CAN, AUS, NZL)

TUESDAY
26

Boxing Day, St Stephen's Day (Holiday UK, R. of Ireland, CAN, AUS, NZL)

WEDNESDAY ○
27

THURSDAY
28

FRIDAY
29

SATURDAY
30

SUNDAY
31

New Year's Eve

JANUARY 2024

MONDAY
1

New Year's Day (Holiday UK, R. of Ireland, USA, CAN, AUS, NZL)

TUESDAY
2

Holiday (SCT, NZL)

WEDNESDAY
3

◑ THURSDAY
4

FRIDAY
5

SATURDAY
6

SUNDAY
7

IMPORTANT DATES

....
....
....
....
....
....
....
....
....
....
....
....
....
....
....
....
....
....
....
....
....
....
....

ADDRESS & TELEPHONE

Name: ....

Address: ....

....

....

Postcode: ....

Telephone: ....

Work: ....

Mobile: ....

Fax: ....

E-mail: ....

Name: ....

Address: ....

....

....

Postcode: ....

Telephone: ....

Work: ....

Mobile: ....

Fax: ....

E-mail: ....

ADDRESS & TELEPHONE

Name: ....

Address: ....

....

....

Postcode: ....

Telephone: ....

Work: ....

Mobile: ....

Fax: ....

E-mail: ....

Name: ....

Address: ....

....

....

Postcode: ....

Telephone: ....

Work: ....

Mobile: ....

Fax: ....

E-mail: ....

ADDRESS & TELEPHONE

Name:

Address:

Postcode:

Telephone:

Work:

Mobile:

Fax:

E-mail:

Name:

Address:

Postcode:

Telephone:

Work:

Mobile:

Fax:

E-mail:

ADDRESS & TELEPHONE

Name:

Address:

Postcode:

Telephone:

Work:

Mobile:

Fax:

E-mail:

Name:

Address:

Postcode:

Telephone:

Work:

Mobile:

Fax:

E-mail:

ADDRESS & TELEPHONE

Name:

Address:

Postcode:

Telephone:

Work:

Mobile:

Fax:

E-mail:

Name:

Address:

Postcode:

Telephone:

Work:

Mobile:

Fax:

E-mail:

ADDRESS & TELEPHONE

Name:

Address:

Postcode:

Telephone:

Work:

Mobile:

Fax:

E-mail:

Name:

Address:

Postcode:

Telephone:

Work:

Mobile:

Fax:

E-mail:

ADDRESS & TELEPHONE

Name:

Address:

Postcode:

Telephone:

Work:

Mobile:

Fax:

E-mail:

Name:

Address:

Postcode:

Telephone:

Work:

Mobile:

Fax:

E-mail:

ADDRESS & TELEPHONE

Name: ....

Address: ....

....

....

Postcode: ....

Telephone: ....

Work: ....

Mobile: ....

Fax: ....

E-mail: ....

Name: ....

Address: ....

....

....

Postcode: ....

Telephone: ....

Work: ....

Mobile: ....

Fax: ....

E-mail: ....

NOTES

NOTES

NOTES